AFTER DESIRE

AFTER DESIRE

George Stanley

VANCOUVER ▼ NEW STAR BOOKS ▼ 2013

NEW STAR BOOKS LTD.

107 — 3477 Commercial Street, Vancouver, BC V5N 4E8   CANADA
1574 Gulf Road, No. 1517, Point Roberts, WA 98281   USA
www.NewStarBooks.com   info@NewStarBooks.com

Publication of this work is made possible by the support of the Government of
Canada through the Canada Council and the Department of Canadian Heritage
Canada Book Fund, and the Province of British Columbia through the British
Columbia Arts Council and the Book Publishing Tax Credit.

Cover by Mark Mushet
Cover image: Mina Totino, *Plink* (detail)
Printed on 100% post-consumer recycled paper
Printed and bound in Canada by Gauvin Press
First published May 2013

Cataloguing information for this book is available from
Library and Archives Canada, www.collectionscanada.gc.ca.

After Desire

2005 – 2011

1971

Open Space

AFTER DESIRE

•

BEAUTY

At a sushi joint I went to infrequently
there was a waiter I called Beauty.

I was tickled by his dark eyes
& his hip-length black apron.
I thought his dad must have been Russian,
he was so tall.

He only ever served me once.

When I'd pass by the restaurant, I'd always look in
to see if Beauty was there.

There was another waiter, looked like Beauty.
Sometimes at first I'd think he was Beauty,
but then he'd come toward the window,
showing some customers to a table,
& I could see it wasn't Beauty.

Sometimes I couldn't tell right away
because of the reflections of cars in the window.
And I was afraid if I peered in too intently,
Beauty would see me, and know.

One night I took Beauty home.
Took? His long legs loped
up the stone steps ahead of me.

I unlocked the door to my apartment
& followed him in.
But when we were face to face,
I didn't know what to do with him.

I didn't want to hurt him
(any more)
I didn't want him to take me in his arms
(any more)
so I let him vanish.

I let him go.

I let him go back to his body.

I let him escape
the violent eye
that fastens on beauty
to possess or destroy.

THE MUSICIAN

for Matthew Jordan

After desire the air lost its voice.

The musician whose black curls were cut
when he went to work in the kitchen
now sits at the end of the bar
in my seat, and I sit perpendicular
to his sadness, watching the game,

and it's class, I tell N., the bartender,
to have the game on, it makes it feel
like a real bar. To go to the bar
& have to pretend it's a real bar.

Not to have to pretend the musician
looks straight ahead in his sadness.
I hear all kinds of voices here,
especially Jack's, always a bad sign,
tells me I'm pretending to write a poem.

Jack would say where are the musician's
black curls? Do you wear one on the corner
of your heart?

And sometimes he doesn't show up
for the Gong Show. If he reads this he would know.

The Phantoms Have Gone Away

The phantoms have gone away
& left a space
for beauty.

And the freedom from desire
leaves a stillness, a moment
when you believe.

This is that moment.
Visions of beauty
in an unfamiliar stillness.

They can be spoken to,
called by name.

Desire will not drag
them home.

JACK

Jack, dead at 40, sees me,
73, in the boring bar, waiting

for something to happen. There isn't even
a game on, just PokerStars.

At the Pub

At the pub I am pretending to drink at the pub, as writing a
poem, I am pretending to be writing a poem. This is a valid
activity. It is something that before I started thinking so
much I thought of as art, or life, or didn't think of at all.

Hard to say what the difference is, between being at the bar,
drinking, having a good time without thinking, and going
now, having to insert myself into that role, sit on that stool,
and think that is a good stool to be sitting on, the act of
ordering a beer, a Pale Ale, a good act, & this role to be a good
role — but not quite the real thing.

But I guess it wasn't the real thing then either. I guess then
I wouldn't have understood the distinction, if it had been put
to me. It must be all this thinking, all this knowing. Being
at the pub then, writing a poem then, was quite apart from
thinking. I didn't think then. I talked a lot, but I didn't
think. But now I think this is all made up but it's all there is
— save the body.

When I drink at the pub I say to myself, I'm drinking at the
pub, & that's a good thing to do. That's the kind of thing
a person would do who didn't think so much. It's good to
write a poem, too, and if there's a phrase, any two words, a
collocation, to consider it, it and its neighbours, the other
words & phrases nearby it in the poem, study them, stare at
them till they stare back, till you're not there any more & they

can move, make the little positional shift something does that's coming to life in a scary world, coming to life to live in that world, maybe to save that world.

The poem I'm pretending to write — is that the poem on the horizon? You'd never know it.

When I drink at the pub I'm pretending to drink at the pub because that's a good thing to do, & when I'm writing a poem I'm pretending to write a poem because those are the conditions of my probation,

but when I ride the bus there's no pretense involved. When I ride the bus I'm just a bus rider.

WALKING SLOW

Walking slow to catch a fair
complexion.

Snuffling after your former prey,
pale cheek & neck, dark curls.
Do you dawdle, stumble over the man
in his bedroll at 1 pm?

Plan a trajectory to give the sleeper
a wide berth. Hop on the bus,
flash your pass, head for the back,
the right corner seat in the last row.

Always on the lookout for a cute kid.
But backs of heads, white earbuds in ears,
caps. Up front, a woman with a stroller.

"How old is he?" There's the community
of women. "Four months."
"Make room for the stroller" (the driver).
"You have to move." So she can sit down
& hold the stroller by the handle & set the brake.

You Want to Imagine

You want to imagine the words you would like to read
that would tell how the world suddenly came apart

more of how the parts, free of their false togetherness,
asserted their separate beings, the world of power without
  qualification,

the reality of pity for the innocent,
your own body & soul, blighted,

words that would grasp this process of disintegration,
  diremption,
as a moment of rebirth —

so the knowledge that no such rebirth is possible is one thing,
the rebirth itself another —

in the city, in lucidity for a moment
on the knife edge between truth (with no qualification)
and meaninglessness. That this observer will go

to one of the hospitals, and the young and
  innocent who have never spoken

a script written for them by power
stay in their moments sharply divided
  from your departure

and which proceed at a hundred perpendiculars
not to arrive at the same destination

no one to arrive at your destination but you
and power goes on,
a reality around your mind
seen as it would be seen, no interior
    knowledge of it visible

just the way the air turns black
with an exudation of knowledge,
    its own oil.

I would like to read the poem
that departs from truth

at the cost of death
invisible to all but by its kindly stature

disclosing opening out
the eternal world where the others live.

　　　•

The passage of desire like a fact.
The heroism of young parents, another fact,
living with desire and with heroism
of care — how can they have been placed
on this precipice — always at the edge of being?

How can the world be so indifferent?
How can they be so indifferent and at the same time

placed at an extreme point, beyond even
 all of their knowledge
and with desire?

Often it is as if everything has stopped
(though everything is moving, the bus is moving)
the heart without desire — is it a heart?
One must begin to gather knowledge
like this — the objects of feeling
 without feeling,
the feeling of others,
second-best heart, Frost's
 diminished thing.

To make use of the feelings of others,
to make of them a cloak, to hide
from the screaming baby in the brain
(a cloak of invisibility
to hide insensibility)

always turn outward
world of heroism and indifference
and persistence, inertia, at the same time
and beauty — the beauty of innocence
even of one's own innocence
before death. Stripped of even the
 desire for desire,

angry at the leaves you track in,

angry at the self you track in.

Home from peeping at the babies,
vicariously enjoying
the plight of the young
    in their extremity
how can you be so indifferent?

·

Les jeunes hommes on their way home from school.
Extinct fantasies.

They come to mind less often now.
Indescribable missingness.

Men and women take their place
(yes, men and women)
(you wouldn't be kidding us now, wouldja Mary?)
and strollers, and you ask, what are babies?
And, what good is a newborn baby
for whom you are already dead.

Electric shock of being looked at by a baby,
suddenly you come into existence, pierced,
then dismissed.
                Pierced/perceived,
and to be perceived is to exist.

(Two generations of kids in the pub, X and Y)

The babies seem to stand up in their strollers
& raise their fat arms & grip
lightning bolts in their fists.

Too much pondering, too much walking
    the streets ruminating
& then noticing, the strings of language
like chopped up DNA —
    the illusion of "thought"
(these babies will wonder what that was)

O mournful. Strike any attitude.
Mark tells me, that's what sucks,
attitude. So to remain quiet & let
thought recede silently beneath perception
like beneath a door.

They are children, they become young
men & women. And at the meeting
my fellow board members' faces grow
more sharp & pointed.

When in the restaurant a baby suddenly looks at me
I see myself in the baby's view —
not there at all, & to recoup,
I look back at the baby
who seems on fire.

To be is to be perceived — by a baby.

The Infant

The infant takes a step & smiles, then turns back to look up at her dad, on the sidewalk outside Olympia.

The infant will live, god willing, in the world to come, will live *into* the world, taking a step, smiling, then look back quick for reassurance.

The world will hold itself ready for her step. The different parts of the world — the doors of the world — will open as she approaches.

Now she finds corridors and now ledges of mountainsides by the sea. All the ways the others live, unknown to them they work together to provide an entrance, a way for the infant.

And soon she is living and making her own way. And far away the police are chasing the bad guys who would corrupt her, and the soldiers are fighting other soldiers, to keep the world open, to keep the world wide, so the children can find the spaces opening wide for their ways.

Their ways through into the centre. Insensibly they lose this sense of making their own ways. They become masters of the partitions. Now they are older and they become the world themselves.

But if at the last moment, the moment of release, I felt
    qualms,
then the qualms would pursue me throughout the rest of the
    day
until the decision had to be made about drinking or not,
to either blot out the knowledge of who I am
or go trembling with it into another night.

Memories of desire, memories of guilt,
of the primal scene of father and son reenacted,
the son now older than the father had been when he died.

Memories of desire, of longing, to repeat
the rite of submission, but with the roles reversed,
the fantasy son now reassuring the fantasy father,
yes, it is all right, for you to touch me, to talk to me that way,
I forgive you, finally.

Memories of desire, that now
do not reawaken. Father, again I forgive you,
says the son who never became a father.

Loss of Desire

It's been hard even to move the pen across the paper,
suspended between the way the world is, presumed, and the
hard to write words, near lies, relating experience.

Not to try to nail it, sentences long or short, bristling with
qualifications, somehow about the way it is, it goes — another
presumption, identity, who could care less?

Shall I slice up the world to offer especially tempting
tranches? The poem is not much of a favourite in competition
for eyeballs.

Maybe mere words . . . It always comes back to wheeling words
(a difficult task, that, Wheeling West Virginia, especially
without wheels. Without inventing the wheel. It comes back
to wheeling words past the eyehole, peephole, of approval.

But the memory is of nothing — what is desire but a sense
of meaning that dwindles, yes loses (lost) tumescence if
you tell a story of it. It was that time, once, recognized, that
some kind of node on a lattice, glowing without light. But
drawn toward it, and the next time called the same thing,
called desire. What was it like? It was almost more like smell
than anything else, even though parts of the body gleam in
recollection and recollection is a sweeping, stuff swept, swept
away (a sweeping generalization) disclosing a shiny spot.
That was it and then every time drawn to it recognizing it as

the same and if not drawn to it but only mesmerized by the idea of it, a blatant lie, a whispering in the ear of passion, that it was there. I don't miss it, I miss missing it. I miss the lack of it, the failure, every time, to grasp anything but the scum of, the edgings of the shiny spot, the passion wound up, discharged, and left with the joke of being left out of it, turned away, turned down, a card, again, not knowing what card (this is bullshit).

Still all I can say is that it was a place,
that desire that made all the difference,
that place that was not the world,
that seemed an ever available recourse,
a fountain to which I could repair —
(that's bullshit). Not a fountain, a dripping faucet, & me down on hands & knees, an old pipe, in the alley, connected to another & to something outside my life (my life seen as one of the numberless figures in single file towards death). A colour out of space (Lovecraft) — it seems so odd to be

without it — out of it — like silence — like a silence experienced by the skin.

Desire for the Self

Laugh in surprise at beauty.
Laugh at your freedom from desire.
The boy boarding the bus may even
flash you a smile: Thanks for not wanting me.

Take this stillness without desire & breathe it.

But there's one boy who won't shrug you off,
and that's the self. Desire wakes at the self,
you follow him home. You look like
one duplicated figure with four legs
trucking down Broadway.

The self sets the pace & you follow,
the step behind keeping step with the step ahead,
the foot, the leg, the torso.
                                        But this guy too
is not playing your game. Turn your self to your face & you
     see
the same patient mocking smile — don't you get it yet?
Step back & stop & feel the stillness & no, the abyss doesn't
     open.
What a joy to stand on the earth, in your own bedroom even,
     & know
your self doesn't want you.

But alas, there's a third, the desirophile,

nervous as hell, next to his reflection
in the bank window, alert to the hint of desire.

And when the desirer goes after the self,
he goes after the desirer. Now it's a six-
legged creature, out of R. Crumb
or Smokey Stover, step after step after step.

And behind the desirophile,
a whole string of desirophiles

After Desire

After desire the springs of longing
dry up, beauty is almost unrecognizable,
astonished that you passed it by. The background
wants to come into sharper focus, by default,
but you know the background.

And football keeps us going too, politics, reports from the
    slave trade.
Always readying ourselves for a funeral — being asked
to real funerals just sweetens the pot —
some kind of game or other always in play.

It's Friday again, time to do laundry.
The world trying to come into sharper focus
has nothing to offer but the impersonal.
Fair enough, but keep the old identity
in your closet, to be trotted out for wear on holy days.

2005 – 2011

•

OKANAGAN WINE

for George Bowering

What does he wear lightly?
His unassumingness.

Wear or carry?
In French or Spanish it's the same:
porter, llevar.

An excellent north Okanagan merlot —
though like other northern regions,
the north is not known for its reds.

Reality is just outside, in the garden,
but lags behind while we enjoy
the wine.

It could be any moment
or any other moment
from Terrace to Jack Spicer's Inland Sea.

At the C's game,
when the fans clap in cadence,
he claps strongly out of time.

Then it's us who lag behind,
eating our peanuts,

while Reality waves a "Go C's" sign
like Delacroix's Liberty.

Keep 'em guessing
forever. Don't say the devil
is in the details (or even god),
say we are.

John Newlove wrote:
"Do not say time flows.
Say: We do. Say: We live."

Keep reality
guessing.

The fans would bring the bridge
down
marching in time.

Stay out of time.

Sidestep
half-assed
absolutes.

Shout anything you want:
"Greater El Centro!"

A fine
north Okanagan merlot,
though the north is not known for its reds.

AFTER AKHMATOVA

for Sharon Thesen

He shows up in my dreams less often now.
I don't run into him everywhere I go.
A low white fog has settled along the road.
Shadows start to race across the lake.

All day the ringing did not stop,
ringing over the wide, ploughed fields,
deafening ringing of bells from St. John's
Monastery bell towers over the fields.

I was pruning the lilac bushes,
snipping off twigs that had lost their blossoms.
Out on the disused military embankment
I watched two monks stroll by.

World, familiar, understandable, tangible,
come back to life for senseless me!
The Tsar of Heaven has healed my soul
with the icy calm of non-love.

•

Yes, I loved them, those late nights at the pub —
the little round tables with beige terrycloth covers
a-tinkle with glasses of cold to lukewarm draft.
The pub overheated, winter blowing outside,
sarcastic laughter at a literary joke,
and my love's quick glance — helpless, shattering me.

•

Everything looted, privatised, sold.
Death's black wing strobed ahead.
Everything chewed up by ravenous boredom.
Why, then, for us, this lovely light?

By day, cherry-scented breezes waft
from a hidden grove in the suburbs.
By night, ever novel constellations glitter
in the deep, clear July skies.

Something miraculous approaches
our filthy, decrepit houses.
No one (no one!) knows what it is,
but we have expected it for centuries.

Being in the Spurious Moment

Watching the mountains
mindful as a Buddhist
from the bus window
coming into Terrace

eyes not always on one view
river islands sandbars
or up to the sky reading,
reading the world.

All the shit & torture images gone
now the organ is gone
that fed sick pleasure back to the mind,
like a character in a Sophocles play
released from the power of a tyrant
rejoicing.

Being in the spurious moment
back to the body after so long wandering
in terror lands of the mind lost
back to the body awakening to being at last
slow thought making easy.

Mountains sloping grey & distant,
farther lighter, nearer darker,
self quietened by looking,

a visible entrance into a feeling
that is out there like the land a patch of air.

The river winding close
to the highway,
body & mind self-involved.
The river pulling away,
a sense of calm

& death refrains for a minute
lets the knowledge fill space
like images of water
different colours different depths.

Being in the spurious moment,
in the body's spurious moment,
love its uncanniness
relax on its bedlessness.

     •

At the Terrace Inn I woke
from the dream of a joke
that was kind and said yes
to the being that rises
from rumpled sheets
to variations on grooming
routines.

     •

A spurious moment.

Unable not
to reflect.

THE PAST

Why could that door not close? Why could that land not
    disappear?
The world is large, what to do, or maybe not to do, aware, no
    problem there.
And as if, as so often, in dream, and in moments of dreaming
    awake,
knowing this, known already, & halfway between thrilled &
    hopeless,
you would want to leap, you would want to lope,
an easy exchange between this & an easier grip on it,
if only the model didn't intrude, the template, the never
    forgotten.

Any change is a change to the given, the already,
the model of right which is the most recent model
that you did wrong by striking out from.
You would incur punishment by just a slight deviation, a
    desire,
desire a pit opening on vertigo,
& your punishment is to return to the model.
Oh why can't that door be closed, & disappear? The past
    sucks
like gravity, like reverse engineering.

Variations on Poems of Rosalía de Castro

for Renee Rodin

1

In the heat of spring the flowers open & breathe.
The restless seeds are dancing in the soil.
In peaceful air the lazy atoms
kiss as they glance, and pass.

The blood of the young blood seethes;
his heart exults, he dares to think
extravagant thoughts: conceives himself
immortal, like a god.

What matter if his dream is all a lie?
He'll be lucky if he dies dreaming,
while the one who cannot dream lives sadly on.

Ah but how fast everything goes in this damned world!
hurled dizzyingly down time.
This morning's bud unfolded is a rose.
Soon all roses will feel summer's hotter breath.

2

Desire sleeps in his tomb,
desiring nothing.

Is it the soul wailing after its loss
or the rock I carry in my heart?

Each pleasure brings concurrent pain,
but to be tormented allures again.

A light flame plays over the skin of my corpse
that breathes yet lest the flame go out.

3

If you cannot listen to your own soul,
what do you expect to learn from others?
Insensata.

If the fountain in your heart has run dry,
dry too will be any fountain you discover.
Insensata.

Stars shine in the sky, but you are indifferent to all
but the one that shone on your birth.
Desdichada.

Flowers bloom all over the earth, but you care only
for those cut and gifted to you.
Desdichada.

4

Mute and ever pallid, the moon,
advancing over the sapphire sphere,
attended by her court
of clouds and stars,
arouses unassuageable memories in me
of untold rancor and suspicion.

Her lucent magical rays
pour such bile in my heart
that I joy in the thought that she, the goddess,
must fall too.

5

A desolate, indefinable shadow
skims across my vision
in pursuit of another shadow
that endlessly flees it.

I don't know its meaning . . . but I sense
its anguish. And I fear, I don't know why,
it will never catch up to the other.

6

Thrown down the cliff,
he fell into the sea.
Hard rocks broke his head bones.
Sharp spines tore his flesh.

And the dark flood poured into his veins,
mixing with his lymph.

A wet mouth lips half open
gave him death's kiss
by blocking the passage to life
of his own parted lips.

Then they woke him up.
Terrified.
Ah, why, why wake up
one who has died?

To see things
again
in perspective.

The Runaway Trolleybus

for Jamie Reid

I was walking down a street on the Eastside
when suddenly I heard crows cawing,
a loud guitar lick, a rumble of far-off thunder,
& before my eyes a TransLink trolleybus flew by.

How I ended up in the right corner seat last row
of that bus is a complete mystery to me,
but I could see through the rear window it left
a trail of fiery sparks across the city.

It rushed like a storm flying into darkness,
it strayed in canyons past the veil of time.
Stop the bus, bus driver, stop, I yelled.
Stop the bus this minute, & let me off.

•

Too late. Already he'd gone past the limit.
Palm fronds hit the windows, we bumped over clouds.
The Fraser, the Columbia, the Sacramento
we raced across on bridges in the sky.

Then there flashed up ahead a bearded face
that cast on us a questioning glance.
Of course, it was the old poet, the one
who died last year on Hornby Island.

Where am I going? Only my slack heartbeat
& anxious mind can give me an answer.
. I want to transfer to the line that runs
to a spa for the soul, somewhere in India.

•

There's the sign, but its letters are dripping blood.
It says "produce market" — yet somehow I know
that instead of cabbages and rutabagas
it's the cut-off heads of the dead they sell here.

Red-shirted the butcher, with a face like an udder.
The head he had just sliced off — was mine.
There it lay in the box along with the others,
in the gory box, on this very day.

Now on a side street past a board fence
a house with three windows and a scruffy lawn.
Stop the bus, bus driver, I cried.
Stop the bus & let me off & mourn.

•

Marie, you lived here, you sang as you worked,
you fed & bathed me when I was young.
Where now are your body & your voice?
Can it be I have forgotten that you died?

You moaned in your room, your face toward the dawn,
while I was out dancing & drinking martinis & wearing

my blue corduroy coat with the gold lining.
And I never came to see you again.

O now I get it — I see that our freedom
is a beam that breaks through a rift in the heavens.
People & shadows stand waiting
for admission to the zoo of the planets.

·

Then a fresh breeze blows along East Broadway.
Familiar buildings seem rushing toward me:
The Lee Building, the BC Cancer Agency,
electric razor building*, Clock Tower at Granville.

It's winter now, the trolley wires are gleaming.
We speed down the hill from Vine to Macdonald.
At Hollywood Manor I can get a drink,
& pray for Marie's soul, & for me a requiem.

All the same my heart will stay forever gloomy,
my breath will be delayed, my step unstable.
Marie, I never knew it was possible
to mourn so late, to love so late.

---

* The building at 805 West Broadway resembles an antique electric
  razor.

Yawn

In mid-yawn I thought:
The soul is the one who yawns.

Don't gaze into the abyss.
Gaze *out*.

6 – Downtown

If I touched your face I would feel only my hand.

Long after Pushkin

Fare well, Nature.

CZESLAW MILOSZ

for Stan Persky

Whether I walk the discordant mall,
or enter a crowded pub to watch the game,
wedged in at the bar amid rowdy fans,
my mind won't let me be.

Once again it gets my age wrong, then corrects me.
It tells me no matter how many of us are still
walking around, we all must descend,
and that just today a friend has been diagnosed.

Gaze on the Lions, snowy or bare,
& know they'll be there, unshakably,
when people have started to forget my name
as I now forget the names of some of my elders.

If with a young poet I discuss his new poem,
some part of my mind already thinks: Farewell!
Take my place, I say. It's time
for me to rot, for you to shine.

I have got into the habit of saying goodnight
to each day, at bedtime, and vale to the years.

But I am incurious as to which calendar date
will be that of my deathday.

Nor do I wonder where I will die:
in downtown traffic, on a ward at St. Paul's,
or will the building manager unlock the door
to find what had been me cold & fallen.

A dead body can neither know nor feel
the trip it takes to be buried or burned.
Yet I recall smiling being driven past
the old Terrace graveyard above the Skeena.

Pushkin envisioned a sunny grave,
a place where children might come to play.
I fantasize a green wave of Nature
rising to overtop the towers of the city.

1971

●

Note for Poets Involved in Trying to Write the Detective Poem

You're at the point in the case where you have on your fingers
Three bodies
One blonde and staring
One bacon and eggs half done & sliding slowly to the floor
& one old woman 20 years ago, & suddenly there enters the
    case
your mind, agile as he steps from the cab,
It's one of those NY cabs with the yellow checkers on it, You
    know
what question you've been asking
yourself in the caves
that narrow back to something
    & slack water, & you pour yourself
& what hangs in the hearts
    of nightmare like
These fingers?

One nightmare you never got over,
    the child's departure, the nailfile of his mother's sister,
One question, the too easy jigsaw puzzle
    settling into place,
One future, black
    & comical
    (Parked on the motel strip
and it begins to narrow around you

(The easy lights go down
(The future in love with guns
with its strength
& ease, & you can't think of the question you once wanted to
    ask yourself
as a child detective.

Something in addition, that other answer
    something that would keep the secrets
    supervenes

The solution of the case being provided by
its awful mother
lost somewhere between Detroit & Kansas City

You drive strangled.

Something's gone wrong. The trickle of water
    What you wanted
as a child and as a detective was a clue
that would lead nowhere,
    that would stay home with you
develop be a person.

But you follow it thru the shifting crowds
without half as much guts as you once had
Nothing has kept faith

Why not keep write to what it's like for a person
Nothing else can have more than half the importance in the
    world
until that's solved — and the detective

finds out the plague is everywhere —
everyone's trying to count his blessings
though in the bars, in motiveless moments,
they lift the world
& keep it suspended, till sleep

London 1971

The White Hawthorn

for Scott

The white hawthorn, its spread, its blossoms and its
   bowers —
It is there, by all the paths we have walked on —
A great bush of it, by the wooden gate
we had to push open to get into the Field
of Moytura, at night, hung over the stone teeth
at the south end of the Circle,
its delicate whiteness
hidden in its darkness
like a climax of stars
in shrunken space.

White hawthorn by the roads
next comes to mind — sprays of it
rising from the hedges
enclosing a road over a hill
between cow-fields. It was in
the presence of white hawthorn
that we learned not to speak.

The woman at Cong
told us not to cut it,
of the danger.

We did not cut it.

My eyes are dry now — all of Ireland
has receded back into a stunned silence —
even that West part of it, enclosed as with black paper
by drunkenness, boredom, and the futile
attempts to feel for each other
we made (like on Sainte-Catherine
in Montréal — I am rushing
through the personal into a resolve
with myself in the abyss I am in —
it is too painful remembering being out of it —
Before, before —

When we traipsed the lanes of Ireland
in happy silence through the white hawthorn

     •

& I am, in a way, trying to get back inside
(the house (of human life (& I am caught
hanging half inside & half outside the window
& I wish I were not climbing
up, but had guts to stay outside
in the fields; I feel slipping away from me
the knowledge of what it is like
being outside, seeing the human habitation
as construct.

     •

We would enter the House of Life as we would
the House of Poetry. The furnishings for each
picked out to be enjoyed, to be admired

& ourselves in retrospect for their choice,
& also the windows, looking out onto the fields
or the burning city, placed
for perspective.

We are flung down the
Broken Tower
happily. But now see us patching up
places to live. Could we not live
out here, recognizing our inadequacy
& our hopes?

•

the petals of the hawthorn
unseen — the universe
strode over in our Seven-League Boots —

the laughter of the fairies unheard

Vancouver 1971

FOR ROBERT DUNCAN

So the law is the walls backwards
if I cross this bridge it will not support my weight
but in the light of the law the walls soften
they dissolve though I cannot dissolve them.

In some fairy stories you have to close your eyes
and walk confidently at the wall, you will pass
through it, open your eyes, and see its
shining other face behind you.

We have to do it
eyes open. The wall outside
is calling to the wall inside
and yet the law is

eyes open.

The wall, the bridge, and the mirror.

This is the wall: *my* anger, *my* pride.
What anger and pride outside have given me
what I call wall to make a form
of my formless rage
at being born, alone,
is a fact to be borne. I would make
that fact *my* wall, but the law says

go alone, defenseless.

This is the bridge: *my* love, *my* poetry.
Bridges were made to cross rivers
but between *my* and the world is a bridge,
clear water rushing under, or filthy.
I would always take you down
under the bridge, in its shadow, to swim,
    and I swim
badly, swim in my badness, or slog in the sucky mud,
get stuck, my way is to show you
love's impossibility, drown you in me,
    but the law is

cross the bridge, weightless,
it is neither me nor thee, it is
a way.

This is the mirror: *my* face, *my* mind
and wonder at what I will give.
Huge and curved, it sweeps out into the room,
giving back a great, stretched, me,
and so it is to me I give, from me I withhold
my caustic, scorching gifts. I don't know
the way through the mirror,
is it by sleep or by sliding,
by turning, or spinning, or falling,
    or dying,
that I can be lost to me for the world?

Vancouver 1971

OPEN SPACE

•

— I'm waiting to write.

— It's like waiting for the bus. You know the bus will come.

— I don't know the bus will come. All I know is there's a sign here that says "bus stop."

— You may have to flag it down.

— I'm not flagging it down. I'm waiting for the bus that stops at this bus stop.

(with Harlan Shore)

MEMORY SUN HEART

after Akhmatova
for Harlan

Summer's sun fades in my memory,
leaves turn yellow.
Wind carries a few aimless flakes
of early snow.

The motionless lake wears a gelid
mirror sheen.
Nothing will ever happen here,
nothing, ever.

Stick outlines of lindens front
a blank sky.
Probably it's best we did
not marry.

Summer's sun disappears from my heart.
Now it's darker.
Likely this night marks the coming
of winter.

The Vacuum Cleaner

I'd almost finished the vacuuming
when the on-off switch (that had been wonky for months)
finally broke. I couldn't turn the machine off,
it was stuck on on. So I finished vacuuming
& unplugged it.   Next week I took it in to the shop.

A beautiful girl
came out from in back.
I handed her the vacuum cleaner
(the power head, that is;
the attachments I'd left at home),
and as she inspected it, we began to talk
in a friendly way — about what
I don't remember, but I recall feeling
that I was not just a customer
to her.

The beauty of girls
and boys
pursues me
wherever I'm going.

Then I had to take my head in — to the clinic.
I sat in the examining room
waiting for the door to open.
Then it did. The young doctor
entered & said, "I'm Jason."

Why do they riot?

They're lonely.

Their souls
are lonely.

(Their selves
are on Facebook.)

COUNTERPOINT

for Pierre Coupey

The task is to attest
to the ground — what abstraction
is abstracted from — the violence
known to the mind
in the mortal world

drawing is fractal
each stroke recalls a wound —
reveals a foliage of wounds

in each gestural figure
some of the truth is retained —
rushing winds convey futility of power —
descending flak evokes the aftermath —

but transformed: heightened,
opaqued for recognition,
or toned down, to be subsumed
in the longer memory

a way of understanding
that is gradual, knowing,
yet still fierce

a battlefield and a garden
a graveyard and a meadow

Insomnia

Papa Soul,
Mama Body,
Baby Mind.
All in one bed,
one head.

Papa wants to dream,
meet angels.
Mama wants to sleep,
then rise,
make waffles.
Baby wants to think,
all night,
all night long.

All night long
he kept them awake,
thinking.
Papa caught the eye
of not one angel.
Mama rose weary,
too weak to make waffles.

This is crazy,
Papa said.
It's not normal,
Mama said.

All of us thinking,
never one of us winking.
We have to get some rest!

So they shut Baby up
in his own little head
& the rest of his life
he lay there in bed,

thinking, thinking,
always thinking.
Never winking,
ever asking:

What were they thinking
when they put me to bed
in my own little head?

WEST BROADWAY

Each of us has his life-world,
meant as the world for all.

EDMUND HUSSERL

Vague abstract thoughts
tinged with dread

struggle to maintain footing on the north bank (sidewalk)

Akhmatova asked how can you look at the Neva
or step onto
one of her bridges

Vague abstract thoughts cut *like sharp wings of black angels*

This river runs both ways
There are no bridges, only crosswalks
monitored by traffic lights, automaated or ped-operated
    ("Push the button!")

No one knows the feelings
Yet not for nothing are they thought to be sorrowful

Raspberry bonfires bloom in the snow (St. Petersburg, 1914)

•

This river runs both ways.

West it flows (up its tributary Tenth Avenue)
to the "uni" (as I've heard one Ontarienne call it).

East it goes to the "Anti-city" (Scott's word)
& a former city planner says
downtown business interests placed obstacles in the way
of development along central Broadway, seeing it
as a potential rival. From the late '50s, it becomes
Vancouver's doctor-and-dentist-land.

Fairmont Medical Building (1959). Look at the windows.
Fourteen storeys of narrow, dark offices.

Panoramic vista — 19th floor of the "electric razor building":
North Shore mountains & the city glittery like a magic island
from the hygienist's chair, until she tips me back.

Thoughts arrive by bus, car, cab,
on ped X-ings cross Broadway,
afoot, w/cane, walker, in wheelchair;
when traffic flows again, cross Willow,
to clinic, pharmacy, lab.

    •

Tall yellow poles skim the wires,
blue trolleybuses sail by
like Swedish yachts.

99-B's travel fast, carry

stolid swaying standing students
like troop transport.

•

Round midnight a dark voice,
a repetitive chant
getting closer on the north bank (sidewalk)
rises in pitch as it nears —
words become more distinct — they are words —

"Fuck Canada! Fuck Canada! Fuck Canada!"
(crossing Balaclava) "Fuck this goddamn country!"

& now it seems an obbligato, muted, of several voices
(as if reproving the dark voice),
coming from the south bank, in front of Timmy's —
"Canada. Canada."

Then from a block further west a voice starts "O Canada,"
missing the tune.

•

Face unlovely
mix of hair & skin
emanating fury
mouth a cave
"[swallowed word] something to eat,"
takes the proffered coin,
"Thanks."

Each one's individual sequel
conceived as "end times"

& out of a confused argument at the pub
comes:
Write Off the Salmon Streams
Pump the Bitumen Through
Maybe China Will Burn Less Coal

•

A chit? — is that it? — or credit slip — from the old
Pulpfiction, that had closed (next to the Hollywood, that had
also closed) I kept in my wallet, thinking that someday I
might wander by the new Pulpfiction (on the south bank, next
to the wine shop) & apply it to the purchase of a book. The
chit was for $4.50.

So one day I did wander by the new Pulpfiction, went in &
quickly found a book, one I had never read, a classic, *The
Epic of Gilgamesh*. The price was $7.95. I took the book to
the counter & produced my chit — half expecting it would
be considered long outdated & therefore discredited. But no
— the clerk acknowledged it as legitimate and so reduced the
price of the book to $3.45. Plus tax, that came to $3.62. I had
a few pennies in my pocket, so as I often do, I gave her two of
these to make the change (from a five) come out even — well,
no, mainly to get rid of them.

As I was handing the two pennies over to the clerk, I noticed

that one of them bore a familiar handsome face — a profile —
it took me back to my childhood — it was King George VI. I
checked the date — 1947. I ponted this out to the clerk, who
said, "Do you want to keep it?" A moment's thought — "Yes."
I put it back in my pocket & came up with another (newer)
penny to give to her.

On my way home now, I stopped off at another bookstore,
Brigid's Books, where my friend Sean was seated at the desk,
reading as always. Happily I showed him the *Gilgamesh* &
said, "If I hadn't found this, I'd probably be browsing here."

Next stop was Parthenon, to pick up some deli items —
Jarlsberg cheese, German salami, maybe Kalamata olives, I
can't recall. The bill came to some odd sum ending in 3 or 7,
and as I had a few pennies in my pocket, I put down two or
three of them to make it come out even — well, no, mainly to
get rid of them.

Two days later: "Where's my 1947 penny?"

They're diverting the Euphrates to build Bilgames' (the
Sumerian name for Gilgamesh) tomb.

"They breached the Euphrates, they emptied it of water,
its pebbles gazed on the Sun God in wonder."

Notes

p. 30. "After Akhmatova" ("Yes, I loved them"). Akhmatova set this poem in the Stray Dog literary cafe in St. Petersburg. I have relocated it to the pub of the Cecil Hotel in Vancouver, early 1970s.

> In Vancouver we had pub night only on Tuesdays.
> Nevertheless the management of the Cecil
> tried to drive us out, first with country music,
> which failed, then with strippers, which succeeded.
> > *'The End of Bohemia?'*

p. 35. "Variations on Poems of Rosalía de Castro." The poems are taken from *Selected Poems: Rosalía de Castro*, translated by Michael Smith. Exeter, UK: Shearsman Books, 2007.

p. 38. "To see things . . ." The last three lines are not in the original poem.

p. 39. "The Runaway Trolleybus." After Nikolai Gumilev, "The Tram That Lost Its Way" (*ca.* 1920). Nikolai Gumilev was a leading Acmeist poet and the first husband of Anna Akhmatova. Accused of conspiracy against the Soviet government, he was shot by a firing-squad in 1921.

p. 44. "Long after Pushkin." An imitation of an 1829 poem by Pushkin, "Whether I wander along noisy streets."

1971. These poems went missing for a long time.

Open Space. I have borrowed this title from the poetry magazine edited by Stan Persky in San Francisco in 1964.

p. 70. Gilgamesh quote from *The Epic of Gilgamesh,* translated by Andrew George. London: Penguin, 1999, p. 205-06.

Acknowledgments

"Okanagan Wine" was included under the title "Unassuming" in *71(+) for GB*, an anthology for George Bowering, edited by Jean Baird, David W. McFadden and George Stanley. Toronto, n.p., n.d. [2006].

"The Runaway Trolleybus" was included in *Can You Hear Me Now?*, a tribute to Jamie Reid, edited by Carol Reid. North Vancouver BC: Blue Window, 2011.

"Counterpoint" was included in a slightly different form in *one more once*, for Pierre Coupey's 70th, compiled by Patti Kernaghan, edited by Jenny Penberthy. North Vancouver BC: Capilano University Editions, 2012.

Thanks also to *Blue Canary*, *The Capilano Review*, *Fras*, *Matrix*, *The Poker*, and *Polis*, and where other poems in *After Desire* first appeared, sometimes in slightly different form.

The author gratefully acknowledges the receipt of grants from the British Columbia Arts Council and the Canada Council for the Arts.